KIRSTENBOSCH

COLIN PATERSON-JONES
JOHN WINTER

**MISSION STATEMENT OF THE
NATIONAL BOTANICAL INSTITUTE**

*To promote the sustainable use,
conservation, appreciation and
enjoyment of the exceptionally
rich plant life of South Africa
for the benefit of all its people.*

INTRODUCTION

Kirstenbosch is one of the world's most famous botanic gardens, and its situation on the lower eastern slopes of Cape Town's Table Mountain is uniquely spectacular. The gardens, which attract some 600 000 visitors a year, are just 40 hectare of an estate that occupies 532 hectare of mountainside. The balance is a nature reserve that supports fynbos, forest and a variety of animals, and extends to Maclear's Beacon, the highest point of the Cape Peninsula. The estate and gardens are managed by the National Botanical Institute (NBI). Kirstenbosch is the largest of the NBI's eight botanical gardens throughout South Afirca.

THE PHILLIPS' LEGACY

The bell hanging in the commemorative tower at the entrance to Kirstenbosch was donated by Lady Sarah Phillips in memory of her husband, Sir Lionel Phillips. Lady Phillips campaigned tirelessly for the establishment of a botanic garden. In 1913 her husband, a Member of Parliament, initiated legislation that led to the formation of the Botanical Society, and the establishment of Kirstenbosch Botanical Gardens.

1 *Bordered with spring annuals, the main walkway into the garden.*
2 *The main vehicle entrance to Gate 2 with 'Pride of De Kaap' (Bauhinia galpinii) in full bloom.*
3 *The gardens and mountain paths are comprehensively signposted.*

Kirstenbosch is ideally situated to showcase the unique plant life of the Cape Flora, both outdoors and in the Botanical Society Conservatory, as well as many different plants from other regions of South Africa. This was the first national garden in the world to be devoted to a country's indigenous plants and includes many important plant collections, including cycads, clivias and succulents. Kirstenbosch enjoys a Mediterranean-type climate with an average rainfall of 1 450 mm a year in the winter and spring. The coldest month is August, with a daily average minimum of 8,5 °C and 16,8 °C maximum. Summers are comfortable, with a daily average minimum of 15,4 °C and 24,7 °C maximum. Strong dessicating south-easterly winds can blow for days in summer, but these are cooling and, fortunately, the garden is largely sheltered.

Kirstenbosch provides the stage for a vibrant summer concert programme, including 'Carols by Candlelight', and for a permanent display of imposing Zimbabwean stone sculpture – a reminder to visitors that they are on African soil.

It is also the starting point for a variety of walks along and up the mountainside, from gentle strolls to more arduous (and potentially dangerous) climbs.

4 *One of the living collections in the nursery.*
5 *A plant researcher in the field, collecting plants for study.*
6 *The plant sales and entrance buildings at the upper car park.*

THE HISTORY

The area known as Kirstenbosch has seen the passage of many peoples and their activities over the aeons. Hand axes and stone implements found in the Dell point to the early presence of Stone Age Man, who must have enjoyed this more sheltered side of the mountain – a mix of renosterveld, fynbos and forest, threaded with streams and rivers. The pastoralist Khoi Khoi arrived here about 2 000 years ago.

KIRSTEN CONNECTION
The name Kirstenbosch first appeared on 18th century maps. Several Kirstens lived at the Cape during this time, including one who was Postholder for the Dutch East India Company land at Kirstenbosch. The name probably derived from this family.

1 *Mr JW Mathews, first curator of the garden, admiring the main pond with the assistant curator, Mr Alec Middlemost.*
2 *Rustenberg School girls arriving for the day's nature study class at Kirstenbosch in 1964.*
3 *Visitors to Kirstenbosch in September 1953 enjoying the display of spring flowers.*

4

In 1652 the first Europeans arrived to settle in the Cape, under the leadership of Jan van Riebeeck. From this time on, parts of the lower slopes of Table Mountain came under cultivation to produce food both for local consumption and for the benefit of passing ships. In an attempt to establish the boundary of the Dutch settlement at the Cape and keep out the Khoi Khoi, Van Riebeeck oversaw the planting of a hedge of wild almond trees in 1670; part of the hedge still grows within Kirstenbosch today – best seen in the treed area above the lawns around the concert stage – and is protected as a national monument.

2

As the number of settlers in the area grew (and local government changed from Dutch to British hands), so did the need for timber, for both fuel and building purposes. Consequently, over a period of about 200 years, the eastern and southern slopes of the mountain were plundered for their indigenous timber: stinkwood, yellowwood and wild olive. To replenish timber stocks, fast-growing trees from Australia and Europe were planted – an activity that would directly impact on the vegetation of the Western Cape in later years. Land continued to be used for forestation and farming until Cecil John Rhodes purchased a wide tract of property on the lower eastern mountain slopes in 1895, with a view to preserving it as a national heritage. On Rhodes' death in 1902, the property reverted to Government land, bequeathed to the people of South Africa.

3

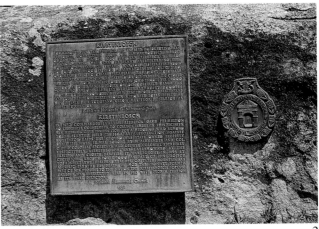

Professor HHW Pearson was sent to the Cape from Cambridge University to become Professor in the Bolus Chair of Botany at the SA College in 1903. He was deeply impressed by the wealth and beauty of the Cape flora, and campaigned for the establishment of a botanic garden. In 1913 the Government set aside the overgrown estate of Kirstenbosch for the purpose of developing such a garden. Pearson was appointed first director of Kirstenbosch, and was to contribute a great deal to the eventual realisation of this dream.

When work started on the garden, Pearson was confronted with 20 years of neglect – there were hordes of pigs in the orchards, buildings from earlier farming ventures were in ruins and the lands were overgrown – and it was from this that he was required to create the order of a botanic garden. In doing so, Pearson was ably assisted by the curator, Mr JW Mathews.

Development started in the 'Dell', its focal point a bird-shaped pond built by a previous landowner. Pearson and Mathews began by clearing the pond and planting yellowwoods and tree ferns. In the natural amphitheatre above the Dell, they planted Pearson's collection of more than 400 cycads. Sadly, in 1916, aged only 46, Professor Pearson died of pneumonia and was buried on the slopes above the Dell.

1 *Professor Compton, then director of the National Botanical Gardens, and Mr Duncan Baxter, chairman of the Board of Trustees, at the official opening of the Mathews Rock Garden in October 1950.*
2 *The National Monuments Commission plaque displayed on an outcrop of Table Mountain sandstone in the Protea Garden.*
3 *The grave of the first director, Professor HHW Pearson, situated above the amphitheatre. His epitaph reads, 'If ye seek his monument, look around you.'*

In 1919 Robert Harold Compton, another distinguished Cambridge man, arrived from England to assume directorship. He and curator Mathews together were responsible for an enormous amount of development. By 1926, some of the principal features in the garden today had been established – the Protea Garden, Cycad Amphitheatre, Erica Garden, the Dell, Mesemb Banks and the Great Lawn.

The interesting and sometimes challenging topography of the area necessitated a great deal of construction work. Dry stone walls, bridges, rockeries, and drinking fountains were all built of Table Mountain sandstone by the local garden staff who, over time, became skilled stonemasons.

As the garden developed, emphasis was placed on building up living plant collections; the cycad collection located in the Amphitheatre is the oldest in the Garden. Other collections in the garden today include proteas, ericas, bulbs, succulents and herbaceous and annual plants.

Early garden development involved the construction of many pathways for easy access. With the installation of an extensive water reticulation system in the 1970s, many of the pathways were removed and flowing lawns were established, which have reduced maintenance and generally enhanced the beauty of the garden.

7

4 *Members of the Board of Trustees admiring the latest development of the Dell in 1919.*
5 *Manoeuvering the baobab tree into position before its planting in the Botanical Society Conservatory in 1995.*
6 *Thatching of the Tea House entrance in June 1996.*
7 *Mr Schreibe, bottom left, horticulturist, being assisted by nursery staff in 1947.*
8 *Jill Scott, then public relations officer, assisting a blind visitor in February 1983.*

4

5

6

8

Financing Kirstenbosch has always been a challenge: in the early days, the Government grant of £1 000 a year was supplemented by the sale of firewood and acorns (as pig food). The Botanical Society of South Africa, launched just a month before Kirstenbosch, has played a major role in the development of the garden by providing substantial financial support. Today, many other projects have been put in place to raise funds, such as plant sales, leasing of facilities, concerts, craft markets and memorial benches.

In the 1990s, with Botanical Society funding, a large capital development programme was launched, resulting in the Kirstenbosch Research Centre, the Botanical Society Conservatory for the display of plants from arid regions, a Visitors' Centre, shops and conference centre, restaurant and, recently, a new tea house plus a Centre for Home Gardening.

THE CAPE FLORA

The natural plant-life in the extreme south-western corner of Africa is very different from any other elsewhere on the continent or, for that matter, in the world. Here, in an area covering just four per cent of southern Africa, is an extraordinary diversity of plants, many of them rare, many growing in only one or two places, and many extraordinarily beautiful. The over 9 000 species of plants found here make up the Cape Flora, and account for nearly half of the roughly 20 000 species in the whole sub-continent. The Cape Floristic Region includes the great mountain ranges, which parallel the Cape's western and southern shorelines and stretch from near Nieuwoudtville in the north down to the Peninsula and eastward to Port Elizabeth, as well as the dry valleys in between these, and the coastal forelands. An astonishing 69 per cent of the Cape Flora's species are endemic (found nowhere else).

1

2

1 *Typical fynbos of restios (Cape reeds) and Leucadendrons.*
2 *Succulent karoo veld on the Ouberg Pass near Montagu, with mesembs in full bloom.*
3 *Cape reeds growing on the slopes of the Villiersdorp mountains.*

Plants of the Cape Flora grow in several different vegetation types. The most widespread of these are fynbos and renosterveld. Fynbos varies enormously, even over short distances, but is characterised by the presence of plants belonging to three families: the protea family (Proteaceae), the Cape heaths or ericas (Ericaceae), and the restios (or Cape reeds) which belong to the Restionaceae. In most kinds of fynbos, restios form the low cover, playing the role that grasses take in the African savanna and grasslands further north.

The protea family includes a bewildering diversity of shrubs, some of which are dominant in certain kinds of fynbos. Ericas, which often grow socially and paint the fynbos veld pink or red when in flower, are mostly small shrubs. Their fine, hard leaves are typical of many fynbos plants. The five richest fynbos families are the daisy family (Asteraceae), the pea family (Fabaceae), the irids (Iridaceae), the Aizoaceae – which includes the mesembs, and the ericas themselves. There are five endemic families in fynbos and three near endemic families. There is an unusually high number of fynbos bulb species, many of them very showy in flower, and some well known in cultivation world-

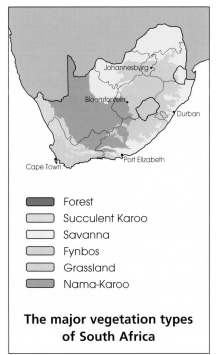

Forest
Succulent Karoo
Savanna
Fynbos
Grassland
Nama-Karoo

The major vegetation types of South Africa

wide. Fynbos covers the leached-out, nutrient-poor soils derived from the sandstone and quartzite rocks of the mountains, as well as coastal sands and patches of limestone.

Renosterveld, which is found on heavier shale and granitic soils where the rainfall is sufficient, has a drab grey appearance because the renosterbos *(Elytropappus rhinocerotis)*, a fine-leafed shrub belonging to the daisy family (Asteraceae), dominates the veld. But this apparent uniformity is misleading – renosterveld has a unique wealth of bulbs that are best seen soon after the veld has burnt. Fire, in fact, is an integral part of the natural fynbos environment, and all fynbos plants are adapted to regular burning. With about 7 000 plant species between them, fynbos and renosterveld account for most of the diversity of the Cape Flora.

In the rain shadow of the Cape fold mountains, the shale soils support a vegetation known as succulent karoo with a wealth of succulent plant species, annuals and bulbs, specially adapted to the long, dry summers. The two other vegetation types of the Cape Flora are dune thicket, and Afromontane forest.

THE GARDEN

Situated on the lower slopes of Table Mountain, a backdrop of great beauty, the developed garden of approximately 40 hectares lends itself to an interesting and informal design. Through the years, the garden has grown in extent and has evolved informally, rather than having been developed according to an overall landscape plan. Readily available natural resources have played a significant role – local sandstone, abundant water and the perennial spring in the Dell. Table Mountain sandstone has become a dominant feature throughout the garden and, thanks to the stone-masonry skills of the staff, features abound, such as walls, bridges, pathways, roads, steps and rockeries to accommodate succulent plants.

THE GIFT OF TIME
The Sundial, situated just above the main lawn, was presented to Kirstenbosch in 1920 by Dr JK Holm, a scientist at the Royal Observatory, whose daughter was employed as a plant recorder at Kirstenbosch.

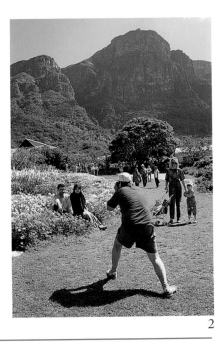

2

1 *Agapanthus blooms in January near the restaurant.*
2 *Visitors among the spring annuals near the Centre for Home Gardening.*
3 *The Silver Tree Restaurant at the lower end of the garden has spectacular views of the garden and mountain.*

1

3

The decision in 1913 to focus solely on the indigenous flora of southern Africa has resulted in the rich diversity of plants reflected in the garden today. A few exotics are also accommodated, some dating back to the days when the area was still a farm, and others, particularly a sampling of tree specimens, that have been donated from abroad.

Prof. Pearson, the first director of Kirstenbosch, established the celebrated collection of cycads in the Dell. Pearson died shortly before an Atlas Cedar arrived as a gift from Kew Gardens. In his honour, it was planted next to his grave, which overlooks the Dell.

Four streams meander through the gardens. The most northerly is Window Stream, which rises at the top of Table Mountain and is crossed by the Silver Tree and Yellowwood trails. Skeleton Stream first appeared on maps in 1811 during the British occupation of the Cape. The pathway alongside the stream (Smuts' Track) is one of three hiking routes up the eastern side of Table Mountain, the shortest and shadiest route up the mountain. Nursery Stream arises south of Castle Rock and is named after the Storr-Lister Nursery (1890), which was used to test the suitability of European trees in the Cape. Each winter, this stream fills the large garden storage dam used to irrigate the garden. The path up Nursery Gorge follows the old mule track, which zigzags, making the route easier but longer. These three streams all dry up in summer. The Dell Stream arises from four perennial springs that feed Colonel Bird's Bath throughout the year, providing crystal-clear water. The water in Skeleton, Window and Nursery streams is tinted brown by tannins from decomposing fynbos vegetation.

4 *Children enjoying the Otter Pond where the waterside plant* Wachendorfia thyrsiflora *is in full bloom.*
5 *A statue of a Cape clawless otter in the pond.*
6 *One of many sculptures from Zimbabwe, which are displayed in the lower part of the garden, north of the restaurant.*
7 *Visitors enjoy the spring display.*

4

5

6

7

Cycads and the Dell

The oldest living plant collection in the garden is of cycads, in which the first director Harold Pearson had a keen interest. They are sometimes called 'living fossils' as they are survivors of an ancient group of gymnosperms belonging to the family Zamiaceae, of which the genus *Encephalartos* is found only in Africa. Cycads, which are dioecious (each plant is either male or female), are wind and insect pollinated. A number of the species in the collection are extremely rare such as **Encephalartos latifrons**, from the Eastern Cape, and **Encephalartos woodii**, which is extinct in the wild and of which only male plants exist. The cycad collection is used for research, education and conservation by making young plants available to the general public and distributing plants to botanical gardens throughout the world.

1

BATS IN ABUNDANCE
On the cobbles in the Dell, you can sometimes find small round 'spit balls' of Cape cluster fig fruits – all in one spot, just below the feeding perch of an Egyptian fruit bat. This is just one of many species of bat that occur on Table Mountain.

2

1 *A view of the Dell with tree ferns,* Mackaya bella *and a large water berry tree* (Syzigium cordatum).
2 *Olive Thrush on the cobbles in the Dell.*
3 *View of the Cycad Amphitheatre with* Encephalartos friderici-guilielmi *in cone in the foreground.*
4 Mackaya bella.
5 *Helmeted Guineafowl on the lawns above the lower end of the Dell, with Fernwood Buttress in the background.*

3

5

4

The natural amphitheatre above Colonel Bird's Bath, the Dell, provided the ideal setting for Pearson's collection of cycads. A previous owner of the farm, Colonel Christopher Bird, deputy colonial secretary, had built the bath some 100 years earlier to capture the crystal clear water from four springs in the vicinity. Shaped like a bird, a pun on his name, the bath is made of Batavian-style tiles, and the rock work was constructed from local sandstone.

Initially the Dell was shaded by oaks, which were gradually removed as the indigenous trees developed. Today Cape holly, water berry and yellowwood provide shade for the tree ferns and other shade-loving plants such as *Streptocarpus* species, clivias, asparagus and *Mackaya bella* that enhance the beauty of the Dell.

The Dell remains one of the most popular parts of Kirstenbosch Gardens, and many visitors make a point of returning to this cool, shady haven again and again.

Erica and Protea gardens

The Erica and Protea gardens, established in 1926, are situated above the Dell in the upper reaches of the garden, and enjoy the cool summer breezes and well drained soils that are ideal for fynbos vegetation. In the early 1970s, both of these features were upgraded and extensive water reticulation systems were installed.

Proteas and ericas are major components of fynbos vegetation, which is adapted to periodic burns. At the age of 10–15 years, many fynbos plants become senescent (old, woody and less floriferous). At this stage in nature, it takes a fire to bring about necessary rejuvenation. In the Kirstenbosch gardens the old woody plantings are removed and replaced with fresh young plants in the autumn in order to maintain healthy and floriferous plantings.

The family Proteaceae is found mainly in the southern hemisphere – in Australia, Africa and Central America. South Africa has 14 genera which include over 360 species, with the greatest diversity in the Cape Flora. *Protea, Leucadendron, Leucospermum, Mimetes, Paranomus, Aulax* and *Faurea* are the main genera displayed in the Protea Garden, which is in flower from winter to early summer. The plantings here consist not only of Proteaceae, but also a wide range of other fynbos plants, such as restios, buchus, phylicas, daisies and legumes to create a natural mix in texture, form and colour.

Ericas in the Cape Floristic Region are hugely diverse, with 625 species recorded. These perennial shrubs range in height from several centimetres to

3

4

5

three metres, and occur naturally in nutrient-poor, acid soils, as well as in limestone and shale soils. Ericas occur in most habitat types from dry mountain slopes or flats to marshes or seeps on hillsides, and some species are found only above a certain altitude.

Ericas are social plants and grow well amongst other fynbos species, such as restios and proteas, some of which are longer lived than ericas and so provide a framework in the garden. Thanks to the wide range of species in the *Erica* genus, there are different types in flower throughout the year. The long-tubed species attract sunbirds, which pollinate them as they probe their flowers for nectar.

6 7

1 Mimetes splendidus *and Castle Rock.*
2 *Pincushions in bloom* (Leucospermum cordifolium).
3 Phylica pubescens *in early summer.*
4 *The queen protea* (Protea magnifica).
5 *The king protea* (Protea cynaroides), *South Africa's national flower.*
6 *The fire heath* (Erica cerinthoides).
7 *A Cape heath* (Erica nana).
8 Aulax umbellata.

8

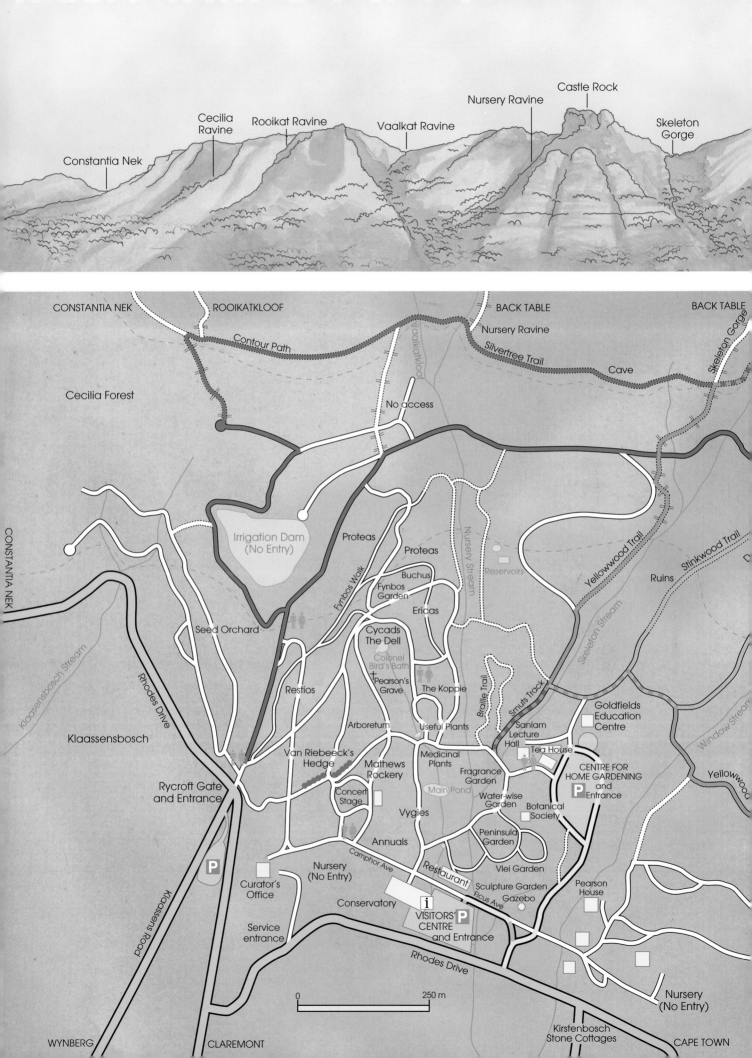

Constantia Nek

Cecilia Ravine

Rooikat Ravine

Vaalkat Ravine

Nursery Ravine

Castle Rock

Skeleton Gorge

CONSTANTIA NEK

ROOIKATKLOOF

BACK TABLE

BACK TABLE

Contour Path

Nursery Ravine

Silvertree Trail

Cave

Skeletan Gorge

Cecilia Forest

Vaalkatkloof

No access

Irrigation Dam
(No Entry)

Proteas

Nursery Stream

Reservoirs

Yellowwood Trail

Stinkwood Trail

Proteas

Buchus

Ruins

Fynbos Walk

Fynbos Garden

Seed Orchard

Ericas

Skeleton Stream

Klaassensbosch Stream

Restios

Cycads
The Dell

Colonel
Bird's Bath

Pearson's Grave

The Koppie

Braille Trail

Smuts Track

Window Stream

Rhodes Drive

Klaassensbosch

Arboretum

Useful Plants

Goldfields
Education
Centre

Sanlam
Lecture
Hall

Van Riebeeck's
Hedge

Mathews
Rockery

Medicinal
Plants

Tea House

CENTRE FOR
HOME GARDENING
and Entrance

Rycroft Gate
and Entrance

Concert
Stage

Main Pond

Fragrance
Garden

Water-wise
Garden

Botanical
Society

Yellowwood

Vygies

Peninsula
Garden

Annuals

Camphor Ave

Restaurant

Vlei Garden

Klaassens Road

Nursery
(No Entry)

Sculpture Garden

Pearson
House

Curator's
Office

Ficus Ave

Gazebo

Conservatory

i

VISITORS'
CENTRE
and Entrance

P

Service
entrance

Rhodes Drive

0   250 m

WYNBERG

CLAREMONT

Kirstenbosch
Stone Cottages

Nursery
(No Entry)

CAPE TOWN

CONSTANTIA NEK

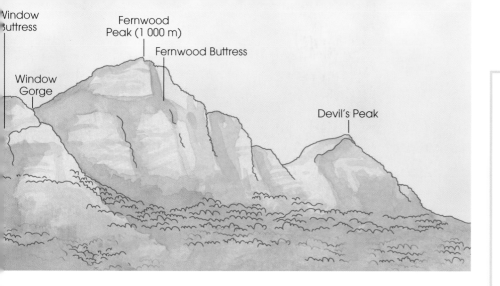

Window
Buttress

Fernwood
Peak (1 000 m)

Fernwood Buttress

Window
Gorge

Devil's Peak

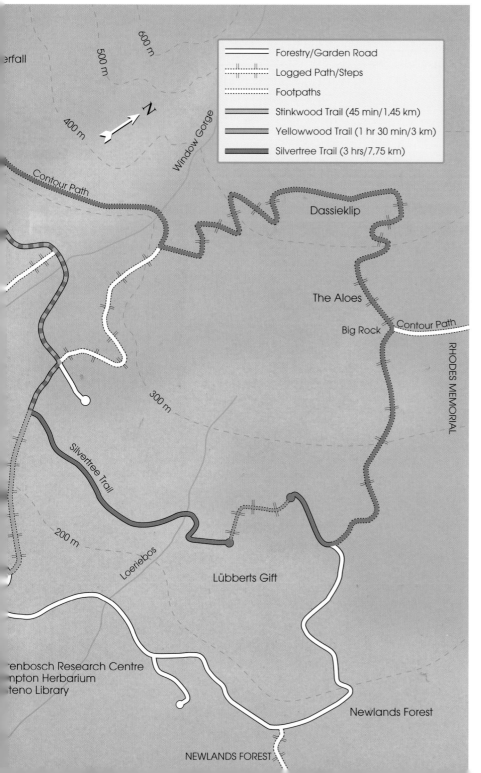

erfall

600 m
500 m
400 m
300 m
200 m

N

Contour Path

Window Gorge

	Forestry/Garden Road
	Logged Path/Steps
	Footpaths
	Stinkwood Trail (45 min/1,45 km)
	Yellowwood Trail (1 hr 30 min/3 km)
	Silvertree Trail (3 hrs/7,75 km)

Dassieklip

The Aloes

Big Rock   Contour Path

RHODES MEMORIAL

Silvertree Trail

Loeriebos

Lübberts Gift

renbosch Research Centre
npton Herbarium
teno Library

Newlands Forest

NEWLANDS FOREST

ACCESS AND WALKS
Kirstenbosch has three access points. The main entrance is from Rhodes Drive at the lower end of the garden and soon divides: left to the Visitor's Centre, and right to the Centre for Home Gardening and Tea House entrance. A kilometre beyond this main entrance is the Rycroft Gate, which provides pedestrian access to the upper reaches of the garden and an opportunity to stroll through the Restio, Protea and Erica gardens on the Fynbos Walk. In addition to the living plant collections on display, visitors have many other options on how to spend time in the garden, one of which is enjoying a variety of trails.

1. STINKWOOD TRAIL
(45 minutes / 1,5 km –
mostly shady)

2. YELLOWWOOD TRAIL
(1hr 30 minutes / 3 km –
mostly shady)

3. SILVERTREE TRAIL
(3 hours / 7,7 km)

Mesemb Banks and the Mathews Rockery

ALOE FEROX

Aloe ferox is a South African plant that has been used medicinally for centuries. It is now sustainably harvested from the wild in the southern Cape to produce medicinal and cosmetic products.

The Mathews Rockery, so named in memory of the first curator of the gardens, James W Mathews (1913-1936), graces the north-facing slope overlooking the main pond. Built entirely by hand, it took several years to complete, and provides an ideal, sunny, well-drained aspect for displaying mesembs, part of southern Africa's largest succulent family, the Aizoaceae. These mesembs flower in late spring, producing a display of every colour imaginable – except for blue. All species have succulent leaves and superficially their flowers resemble daisies. The fruit capsule is essential for identifying mesembs, as almost all are hygrochastic: the capsules are closed when dry and open only when it rains, thus dispersing their seed – an adaptation to their arid natural habitat.

The mesembs displayed here are from the more arid regions of South Africa and, with the high rainfall at Kirstenbosch, only certain species can successfully be grown here for display. They need to be replaced every three to four years. Other plants on display range from bulbs to shrubs and small trees. *Euphorbia* and *Aloe* species are prominent, the aloes providing much colour in the winter months.

1

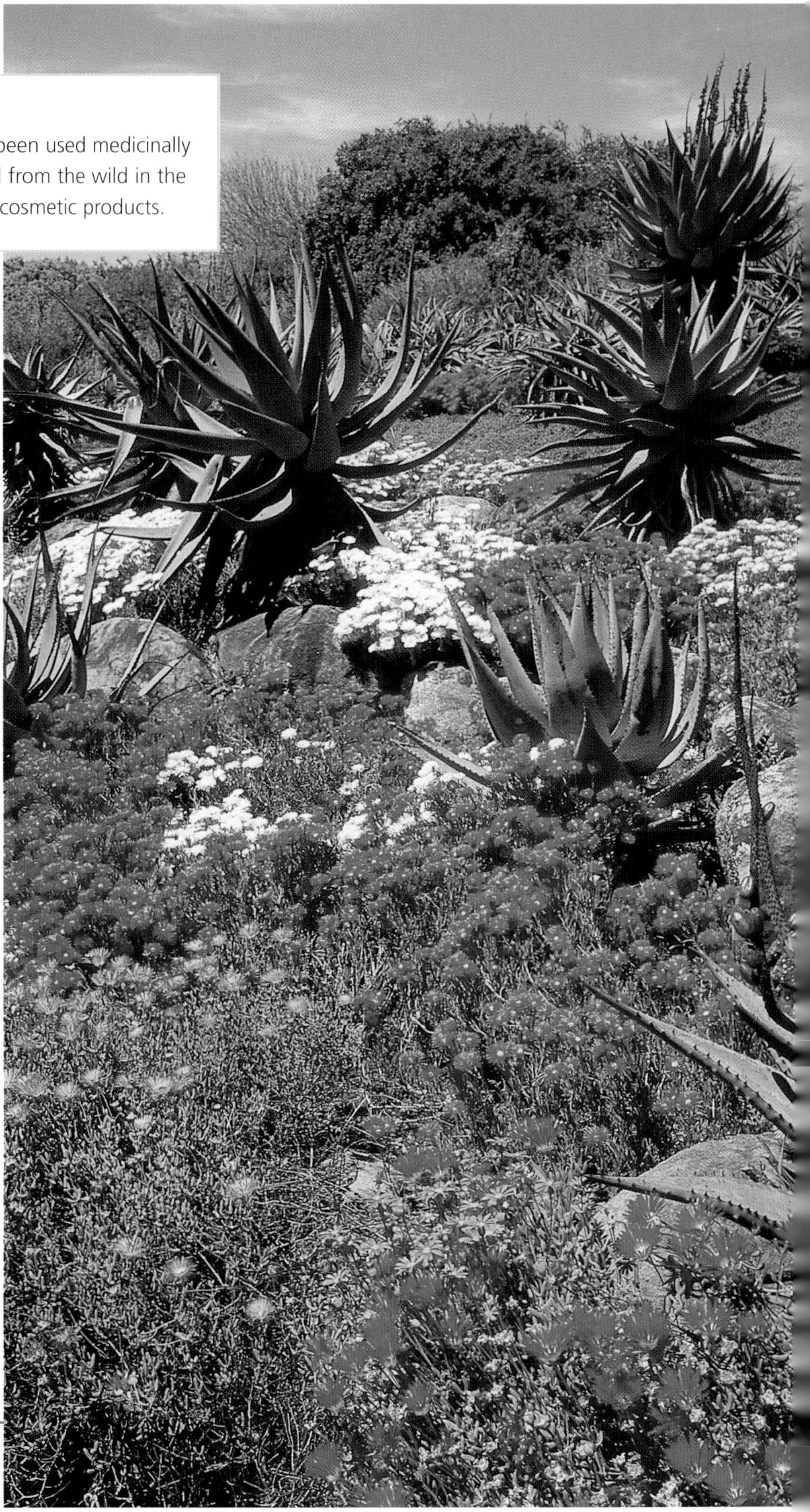

1 *The Mesemb Banks in full bloom in late spring, interplanted with* Aloe ferox, *which flowers in the winter.*

Restio Garden

The restios (or Cape reeds) belong to one of three characteristic fynbos families, and are evergreen, reed-like plants. The Restio Garden was developed in 1992 to create public awareness of restios and to serve as a trial ground for the selection of species with horticultural potential.

Restios are found growing throughout the Cape Floristic Region in poor, sandy soils on the flats as well as in the mountains. About 300 species are endemic, and 57 are considered threatened in the wild. They vary in height from 100 millimetres to over 3 metres. Some of the better known species are *Elegia capensis*, and the thatching reeds, *Thamnochortus insignis* and *Chondropetalum tectorum*.

In recent years, restios have created much interest in the horticultural industry worldwide. Although their individual flowers are tiny and unspectacular, their appeal lies in their form, texture and foliage colour, and the long-lasting seed heads of the female plants are particularly sought after.

The Restio Garden provides an attractive landscape linking the Rycroft Gate with the Protea Garden.

2 *A low-growing restio,* Elegia stipularis.
3 *A small grey mongoose, a shy garden resident.*
4 *A view of young plantings in the Restio Garden.*

RESTIO GARDEN
RESTIOTUIN

The Conservatory and Camphor Avenue

Built with funds raised by the society, the Botanical Society Conservatory opened in August 1996. It was designed by architect Julian Elliott to provide a public display area, sheltered from the rain, with free air circulation and light shade for the well-being of the large collection of succulents, bulbs, alpine flora and ferns that cannot grow satisfactorarily in the garden. Most importantly, the Conservatory was built not to keep plants warm, but to keep them dry. Of the approximately 10 000 known species of succulent plants world-wide, 47 per cent are found in South Africa. Many South African succulents grow naturally in arid areas and would not flourish outdoors on this wet side of Table Mountain. Consequently the greater part of the Conservatory is devoted to succulents, including the world's largest succulent, the baobab tree. The Conservatory is open on three sides to allow free air circulation; these sides are covered with wire mesh, which keeps birds out (as they can damage some plants), but which lets the insects in, as these are needed for flower pollination.

1

1 *The Botanical Society Conservatory.*
2 *The Kay Bergh Bulb Collection displaying bulbs in flower, including several forms of the red disa* (Disa uniflora).
3 *A Maiden hair tree* (Gingko biloba), *displayed in the Evolution Garden.*

2

3

4

The Camphor Avenue runs along a route which, in the early days of European settlement, used to be known as the 'wa-pad', and was probably used for carts dragging timber from the forests to the settled areas. In 1898, hoping to create a British Empire Avenue along his favourite horse-riding route on which the Queen of England would travel, Rhodes planted scores of camphor trees from Hong Kong, Moreton Bay figs from Australia, and cork oaks from Gibraltar. Today, these trees remain, and terraced beds on either side of the avenue are filled with many shade-loving plants such as clivias, asparagus, as well as species of *Streptocarpus*, *Plectranthus*, *Veltheimia*, *Crinum* and *Scadoxus*, which provide colour and interest throughout the year.

5

6

4 *The Camphor Avenue provides a canopy for a range of colourful shade-loving plants throughout the spring, summer and autumn.*
5 *Spotted Eagle Owl chicks in the fork of a camphor tree.*
6 *Visitors enjoying a picnic on the lawns at Kirstenbosch at one of the Summer Sunset Concerts.*

The Main Lawn and Pond

The main lawn, established when the area was first cleared in 1913, is a central point of the garden below Castle Rock. The lawns were all originally planted with 'Buffalo', a hardy coastal grass. However, 'Kikuyu', an aggressive grass originally from the highlands of Kenya has gradually taken over many of the lawned areas.

In 1916 the pond was created in the main lawn, fed by water that flows from Colonel Bird's Bath through the Dell and down the centre of the main lawn. Some of the aquatic plants that can be seen in the pond in summer are the Cape waterlily with flat leaves that float on the surface and with large, blue, star-like flowers; *Nymphoides indica*, which produces small yellow flowers; and vlei lily *(Crinum campanulatum)* with tall spikes bearing pink flowers.

Two large oak trees on the main lawn are remnants from the days when Kirstenbosch was still a farm. In late winter and early spring, the lawns are splashed with colourful oxalis blooms of pink and white.

1 *The main pond displaying Cape waterlilies and 'waterblommetjies'* (Aponogeton distachyos).
2 Dissotis princeps *on the lower main lawns.*
3 *A dung beetle moving its load across the grass.*

The Forest

To many visitors, the 500 hectares of natural fynbos and forest that surround the garden on the eastern slopes of Table Mountain is what makes Kirstenbosch unique. The contour path, which was cut in 1913 on the mountain slopes, approximately 100 metres above the garden, provides visitors with the opportunity of walking in cool, moist, evergreen Afromontane forest and enjoying the views of False Bay as they stroll through the fynbos between the gorges.

Some of the more common trees are the yellowwood, keurboom, a pioneer tree found on the verges of the forest, and ironwood. The well-known stinkwood, felled extensively for furniture by early settlers, is rapidly re-establishing in the forest.

The forest occurs in Window, Skeleton and Nursery gorges, as well as on Lubbert's Gift (see map, page 17), where the conditions are cool, moist and sheltered from the prevailing winds. In winter and spring the streams in the gorges flow strongly but soon reduce to a trickle and can dry up completely in summer.

4

4 *Keurboom, a pioneer tree on forest margins.*
5 *The Cape river frog.*
6 *Leaves in the brown-coloured water of the streams.*
7 *Natural forest on the slopes above the gardens.*

5

6

7

Spring

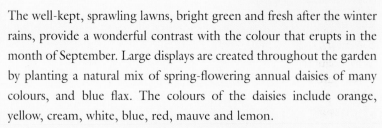

The well-kept, sprawling lawns, bright green and fresh after the winter rains, provide a wonderful contrast with the colour that erupts in the month of September. Large displays are created throughout the garden by planting a natural mix of spring-flowering annual daisies of many colours, and blue flax. The colours of the daisies include orange, yellow, cream, white, blue, red, mauve and lemon.

In the upper reaches of the garden, the pincushions are in full bloom in the Protea Garden, providing bright splashes of orange to yellow that attract sugarbirds.

Numerous other species provide colour in the garden at this time, such as the orange bird of paradise flowers (*Strelitzia*), or a variety with yellow flowers that is known as 'Mandela's gold'; wild iris (*Dietes* species) with yellow or white flowers; and tall aristeas with dark blue flowers that last just a day but are replaced each morning with a display of fresh blooms.

1 *Gousblom* (Arctotis hirsuta).
2 *A mix of spring daisies.*
3 *A male flowerhead of the silver tree* (Leucadendron argenteum).
4 Strelitzia juncea.
5 *Spring daisies.*
6 *The pincushion* (Leucospermum erubescens).

Summmer

7 *Cape chestnut.*
8 Geranium incanum.
9 *Wild Almond* (Brabejum stellatifolium).
10 Crinum moorei.
11 *Pom pon tree.*
12 *Agapanthus.*

The availability of water and a computerised water reticulation system throughout the garden keeps Kirstenbosch looking like an oasis in the hot, dry months from December to February. Trees and shrubs from the summer rainfall regions thrive: *Gardenia thunbergia* produces fragrant, creamy-white flowers in the Dell, while *Buddleja salviifolia* is covered with clusters of tiny pale magenta flowers that add fragrance to the lower part of the gardens. The Cape chestnut produces clusters of pink, scented flowers, which contrast well with the dark green leaves of the tree. The pom pon tree is covered with pink flowers.

Alongside Smuts' track, in damp patches, *Wachendorfia thyrsiflora* thrives, with its tall spikes of golden-yellow flowers. The wild almond has clusters of cream-coloured flowers. In shady areas, the bulbous amaryllid *Crinum moorei*, produces tall spikes with large white flowers, and the subtropical *Scadoxus multiflorus* subsp. *katharinae*, another bulb, displays a large ball of reddish flowers set well above the leaves. As a ground cover, wild geranium spreads and produces a profusion of pink flowers on the edge of beds. *Agapanthus* cultivars are grown throughout the garden, providing spectacular displays of colour ranging from white to many shades of blue.

Autumn

Autumn (March to May) brings cooler, yet more settled weather. Plant growth starts slowing down, and autumn-flowering plants, such as the Cape honeysuckle and *Plectranthus* species come into bloom. The leaves of the deciduous maiden hair tree above the cycad amphitheatre turn a golden yellow and soon blow away in the wind. The evergreen Cape honeysuckle comes into abundant flower, ranging from orange, pink and yellow to red. The Zimbabwe creeper, above the main pond, produces showy, pink, trumpet-shaped flowers against its vigorous, evergreen leaves.

In the main pond, the Cape waterlily sends up stems with showy blue flowers. *Streptocarpus* species found in the shade of Camphor Avenue and in the Dell display large, pale blue flowers. Many forms of plectranthus bloom in the shady areas of the garden, ranging from ground cover to 1,5 metres in height, their flowers in all shades of white, pink and blue. *Lobelia valida* grows in full sun and produces dark blue flowers, which attract insects such as the Citrus Swallowtail Butterfly.

1 *Maiden hair tree* (Gingko biloba) *above the Dell.*
2 *Cape honeysuckle* (Tecoma capensis).
3 Streptocarpus *species.*
4 *Zimbabwe creeper* (Podranea brycei).
5 *Cape waterlily* (Nymphaea nouchali).
6 *Plectranthus.*
7 *Citrus swallowtail butterfly on* Lobelia valida.

8

9

13

8 Leucadendron salignum.
9 *The arum lily, a popular cut flower.*
10 Protea *cultivar 'Pinita'*.
11 Chasmanthe aethiopica.
12 Erica hirtiflora.
13 Oxalis purpurea.
14 Aloe arborescens *and Castle Rock*.

12

10

Leucadendron salignum in the Protea and Erica gardens produces colourful leaves of yellow to copper from June to August; and, looking up towards the slopes of the mountain, are sheets of pink – *Erica hirtiflora* in full bloom.

The *Protea* cultivar 'Pinita' flowers prolifically at this time of the year. An increasing number of cultivars are being produced for cut-flowers and for display in gardens. *Chasmanthe aethiopica*, a bulb with spikes of orange flowers, occurs naturally throughout the garden. On the lawns are patches of oxalis with pink or white flowers that open on sunny days and brighten up the scene. *Aloe arborescens* in the Mathews Rockery presents a dazzling display of masses of orange flowers that blaze against the backdrop of Castle Rock.

11

14

Cecilia Ravine

Rooikat Ravine

Vaalkat Ravine

Castle Rock

Nursery Ravine

Contour Path

Irrigation Dam

Nursery

Botanical Society Conservatory

THE MOUNTAIN

Table Mountain is magnificent and most inviting, especially on a clear sunny day. But beware – every year climbers and hikers are involved in accidents (sometimes fatal), which could have been avoided had necessary precautions been taken. The only popular and safest routes to the top of the mountain from Kirstenbosch are Skeleton Gorge and Nursery Ravine. The Contour Path, set at about 100 metres above the garden, provides access from Constantia Nek in the south and Rhodes Memorial to the north.

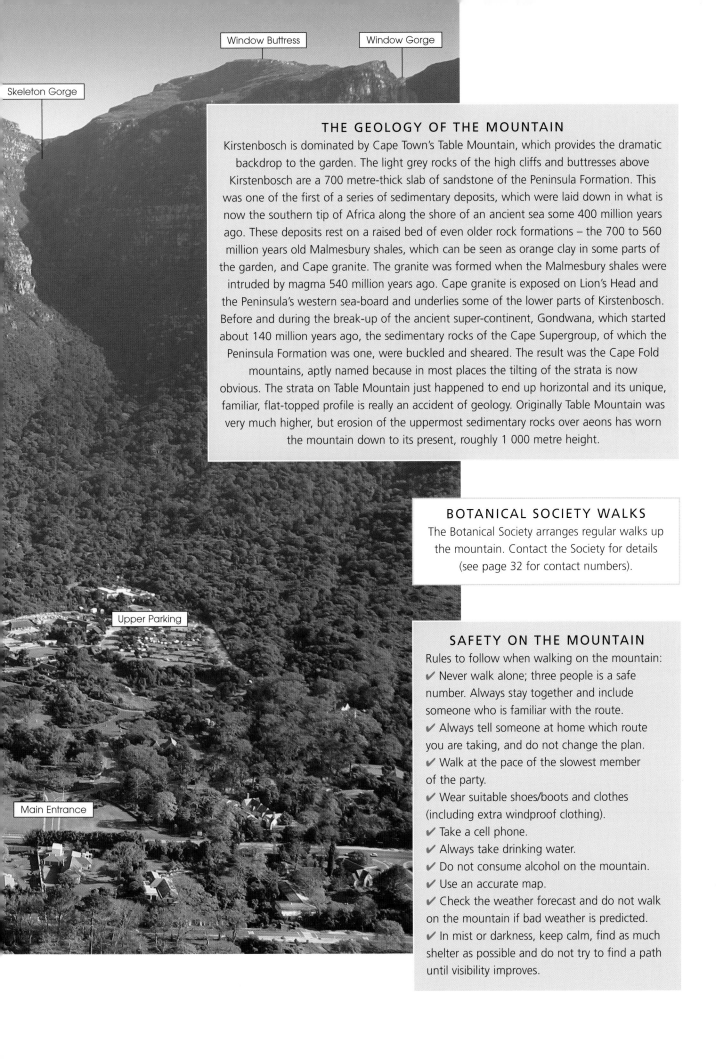

Window Buttress

Window Gorge

Skeleton Gorge

THE GEOLOGY OF THE MOUNTAIN

Kirstenbosch is dominated by Cape Town's Table Mountain, which provides the dramatic backdrop to the garden. The light grey rocks of the high cliffs and buttresses above Kirstenbosch are a 700 metre-thick slab of sandstone of the Peninsula Formation. This was one of the first of a series of sedimentary deposits, which were laid down in what is now the southern tip of Africa along the shore of an ancient sea some 400 million years ago. These deposits rest on a raised bed of even older rock formations – the 700 to 560 million years old Malmesbury shales, which can be seen as orange clay in some parts of the garden, and Cape granite. The granite was formed when the Malmesbury shales were intruded by magma 540 million years ago. Cape granite is exposed on Lion's Head and the Peninsula's western sea-board and underlies some of the lower parts of Kirstenbosch. Before and during the break-up of the ancient super-continent, Gondwana, which started about 140 million years ago, the sedimentary rocks of the Cape Supergroup, of which the Peninsula Formation was one, were buckled and sheared. The result was the Cape Fold mountains, aptly named because in most places the tilting of the strata is now obvious. The strata on Table Mountain just happened to end up horizontal and its unique, familiar, flat-topped profile is really an accident of geology. Originally Table Mountain was very much higher, but erosion of the uppermost sedimentary rocks over aeons has worn the mountain down to its present, roughly 1 000 metre height.

BOTANICAL SOCIETY WALKS

The Botanical Society arranges regular walks up the mountain. Contact the Society for details (see page 32 for contact numbers).

Upper Parking

Main Entrance

SAFETY ON THE MOUNTAIN

Rules to follow when walking on the mountain:
✔ Never walk alone; three people is a safe number. Always stay together and include someone who is familiar with the route.
✔ Always tell someone at home which route you are taking, and do not change the plan.
✔ Walk at the pace of the slowest member of the party.
✔ Wear suitable shoes/boots and clothes (including extra windproof clothing).
✔ Take a cell phone.
✔ Always take drinking water.
✔ Do not consume alcohol on the mountain.
✔ Use an accurate map.
✔ Check the weather forecast and do not walk on the mountain if bad weather is predicted.
✔ In mist or darkness, keep calm, find as much shelter as possible and do not try to find a path until visibility improves.

Birdlife

The gardens provide an ideal opportunity for visitors to observe some common bird species. At the same time, they cater for the more serious birder who is on the lookout for the Cape's endemic species.

Diverse habitats within the gardens provide for a good selection of bird species and, with limited effort, a variety of birds can be observed. Although not all species are restricted to particular habitats, some frequent and are more easily observed in particular areas of the garden.

Developed section: Most common garden species can be observed in the developed areas of the garden. Helmeted Guineafowl patrol the manicured lawns, while Olive Thrush and Cape Robin-Chat seek refuge in the thickets and flowerbeds. The active Karoo Prinia with its long tail and buzzing call can be observed at close quarters, and groups of Speckled Mousebird are a common sight. The Sombre Bulbul with its piercing whistle can be tricky to see in dense foliage, in contrast to the active Cape White-eye. Camphor Avenue is worth searching for roosting Spotted Eagle Owls, a common breeding resident in the garden.

1 *Cape Canary.*
2 *Cape Grassbird.*
3 *Cape Robin-Chat.*
4 *Spotted Thick-knee (Dikkop).*
5 *Cape Sugarbird.*
6 *Karoo Prinia.*
7 *Male Orange-breasted Sunbird.*
8 *Helmeted Guineafowl.*
9 *Cape Francolin.*
10 *Egyptian Goose.*
11 *Male Lesser Double-collared Sunbird.*
12 *Cape Turtle Dove.*

Protea section: This section of the garden is a must for the more serious birder because the Cape Sugarbird (a fynbos endemic), Cape Bulbul, Cape Francolin and exquisite Orange-breasted Sunbird (another fynbos endemic) are all easily found here. The Cape Siskin is also occasionally seen foraging in the proteas, while the distinctive calls of the Grassbird and Southern Boubou are commonly heard.

Indigenous forest: A slow walk along the forest trails of the gardens will reveal the Cape Batis, Paradise Flycatcher (in summer), Forest Canary and Cinnamon Dove. The Knysna Warbler is occasionally heard (though rarely seen), and is best observed towards the top of Skeleton Gorge. Dusky Flycatchers are commonly seen hawking insects from a favourite perch, while the Rameron Pigeon is an attractive species that can often be seen raiding fruiting trees.

Raptors are well represented, with the African Goshawk, Redbreasted Sparrowhawk and Black Sparrowhawk all being regularly seen. In season, the migratory Steppe Buzzard can be seen, and is not to be confused with the Forest Buzzard, which is an uncommon resident species that can also be spotted in the summer months.

Struik Nature
(an imprint of Random House Struik (Pty) Ltd)
Reg. No. 1966/003153/07
80 McKenzie Street, Cape Town, 8001
PO Box 1144, Cape Town, 8000 South Africa

Visit us at **www.randomstruik.co.za**.
Log on to our photographic website
www.imagesofafrica.co.za for an
African experience.

First published in 2004

3 5 7 9 10 8 6 4

Copyright © in text, 2004: John Winter
Copyright © in photographs, 2004: Colin
Paterson-Jones, with the exception of the
following: pp 1 (top), 4 (left), 5, 6 (top left), 7
(top left & right, bottom right) – Harry Molteno
Library/NBI;
p 4 (map) – NBI; pp 9, 16-17 (maps) – copied
with permission of NBI;
p 21 (bottom right) – Chanan Weiss/SIL; pp
28-29 – Anthony Allen.

Copyright © in maps, 2004:
Random House Struik (Pty) Ltd
Copyright © in published edition, 2004:
Random House Struik (Pty) Ltd

Publishing manager: Pippa Parker
Editor: Helen de Villiers
Designer: Janice Evans
Cover design: Janice Evans
Cartographer: David du Plessis

Reproduction by
Hirt & Carter Cape (Pty) Ltd
Printed and bound by
Times Offset (M) Sdn Bhd

ISBN 978 1 86872 937 1

*Spring daisies below the
Sanlam lecture hall.*

Disa uniflora.

The author acknowledges
with thanks the assistance and
support of the staff at NBI.

KIRSTENBOSCH BOTANICAL GARDEN
Private bag X7, Claremont, 7735 South Africa
Tel: 27 21 799-8899
Fax: 27 21 797-6570
Web address: **http://www.nbi.ac.za**

NATIONAL BOTANICAL INSTITUTE
Private bag X7, Claremont, 7735 South Africa
Tel: 27 21 799-8800
Fax: 27 21 761-4687
Web address: **http://www.nbi.ac.za**

BOTANICAL SOCIETY OF SA
Private bag X10, Claremont, 7735 South Africa
Tel: 27 21 797-2090
Fax: 27 21 797-2376
E-mail: info@botanicalsociety.org.za
Web address: **http://www.botanicalsociety.org.za**